Destination Detectives

Japan

North America

Europe

Asia

Africa

South America

JAPAN

Australasia

Jen Green

Raintree

Chicago, Illinois

Printed and bound in China WKT Company Limited

10 09 08 07 06
10 9 8 7 6 5 4 3 2 1

**Library of Congress Cataloging-in-
Publication Data**
Green, Jen.
  Japan / Jen Green.
    p. cm. -- (Destination detectives)
  Includes bibliographical references.
  ISBN 1-4109-1865-3 (library binding-hardcover)
  1. Japan--Juvenile literature. I. Title. II. Series.
  DS806.G6 2006
  952--dc22
                                      2005011558

Acknowledgments
The author and publishers are grateful to the following
for permission to reproduce copyright material:
Alamy Images pp. 14–15 (A M Corporation), 16–17 (David
Pearson), 39 (Hideo Kurihara); Corbis pp. 33 (B.S.P.I.), pp.
10–11, 11r (Bettmann), pp. 5t, 18–19 (Charles & Josette
Lenars), 32 (David Samuel Robbins), pp. 21l , 41t (Free Agents
Limited), pp. 5m, 26 (Kim Kyung-Hoon/Reuters), 30–31
(Kimimasa Mayama/Reuters), 34–35 (Michael Boys), 9
(Michael Maslan Historic Photographs), pp. 6, 14, 26–27,
36–37 (Michael S.Yamashita), 12–13 (Peter Guttman), pp. 13,
41b (Reuters), 28 (Richard T. Nowitz), 38 (Robert Essel
NYC), 31t (Roger Ressmeyer), pp. 5b, 43b (Steve Kaufman),
8–9 (Werner Forman); Exile Images pp. 24–25 (J.Holmes);
Getty Images p. 23 (Photodisc); Harcourt Education Ltd pp.
4r, 4l, 7, 17t, 20, 21r, 24t, 25t, 34, 36 (Debbie Rowe); JNTO
pp. 18, 28–29, 42; Robert Harding Picture Library pp. 5
(Chris Rennie), 22 (P Koch); Travel-Ink p. 43t (Andy Lovell).

Cover photograph of colourful Japanese lanterns reproduced
with permission of Corbis/ Michael S. Yamashita.

Illustrations by Kamae Design.

Every effort has been made to contact copyright holders of
any material reproduced in this book. Any omissions will be
rectified in subsequent printings if notice is given to the
publishers.

The paper used to print this book comes from
sustainable resources.

Disclaimer
All the Internet addresses (URLs) given in this book were valid
at the time of going to press. However, due to the dynamic
nature of the Internet, some addresses may have changed, or
sites may have changed or ceased to exist since publication.
While the author and publishers regret any inconvenience this
may cause readers, no responsibility for any such changes can
be accepted by either the author or the publishers.

Contents

Some words are shown in bold, **like this**. You can find out what they mean by looking in the glossary. You can also look out for them in the Word Bank box at the bottom of each page.

Where in the World?

Dangerous Beauty

Beautiful Mount Fuji is Japan's most famous landmark and highest mountain at 12,385 feet (3,776 meters) above sea level. But Fuji's snowy cone hides danger. The mountain is a volcano that has been quiet for 300 years but has recently shown signs of erupting again.

You awake to find yourself in a room unlike any you've ever been in. You are snug on a **futon** on a large straw mat on the floor. There's very little furniture in the room, but a print of a cone-shaped mountain hangs on the wall. Is this a clue to where you are?

Out of the window you can see an interesting garden—a tiny yard with a single tree and neatly raked gravel. Beyond that there's a park with cherry trees and what looks like a **pagoda**. Surely this must be Japan!

WORD BANK   futon   mattress that can be rolled up when not in use

Welcome to Japan

You become aware of muffled laughter outside your room. What you thought was a wall turns out to be a screen. It slides back, and behind it you see a girl of about your age, with black hair and Asian features. "*Yokoso*—welcome; to Japan," she says. She introduces her family and explains that you are in a *minshuku*. This is a home that takes paying guests. You're in the Japanese city of Kyoto.

Japanese homes are small and simply furnished. People sit on cushions around a low table instead of using chairs and a table.

Japanese Names

When Japanese people introduce themselves, the family name comes first, then the first name.

Find Out Later...

What is **Kabuki**?

How much does an average *rikishi* (**sumo** wrestler) weigh?

What types of wildlife can you find in Japan?

pagoda tall, tower-like temple with several layers of curving roofs

So what do you know about Japan? Over breakfast your hosts tell you a lot with the help of a map and vacation photos.

Where is Japan?

Japan is in Asia and is located in the northwest Pacific. Russia, China, and Korea lie about 310 miles (500 kilometers) away to the west, with Canada and the United States 4,350 miles (8,000 kilometers) to the east across the ocean. With more than 125 million people, Japan is a densely populated country. This means that many people live close together on a small area of land.

Four main islands

Japan is mainly made up of four large islands: Hokkaido, Honshu, Shikoku, and Kyushu. Kyoto is on the largest island, Honshu, which is often called the mainland.

Workers assemble the electronic parts of a high-tech toilet in one of Kyushu's modern factories.

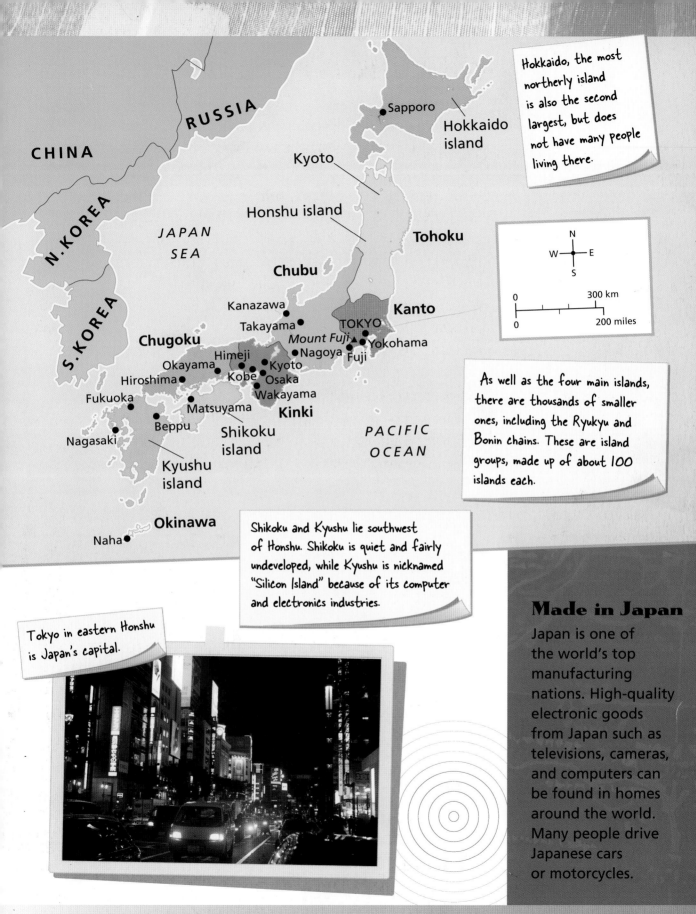

RUSSIA

CHINA

N. KOREA

S. KOREA

JAPAN SEA

Sapporo

Hokkaido island

Kyoto

Honshu island

Tohoku

Chubu

Kanto

Kanazawa

Takayama

TOKYO

Mount Fuji

Yokohama

Nagoya

Fuji

Chugoku

Himeji

Okayama

Kyoto

Hiroshima

Kobe

Osaka

Fukuoka

Wakayama

Matsuyama

Kinki

Beppu

Shikoku island

PACIFIC OCEAN

Nagasaki

Kyushu island

Okinawa

Naha

N
W — E
S

0 — 300 km
0 — 200 miles

Hokkaido, the most northerly island is also the second largest, but does not have many people living there.

As well as the four main islands, there are thousands of smaller ones, including the Ryukyu and Bonin chains. These are island groups, made up of about 100 islands each.

Shikoku and Kyushu lie southwest of Honshu. Shikoku is quiet and fairly undeveloped, while Kyushu is nicknamed "Silicon Island" because of its computer and electronics industries.

Tokyo in eastern Honshu is Japan's capital.

Made in Japan

Japan is one of the world's top manufacturing nations. High-quality electronic goods from Japan such as televisions, cameras, and computers can be found in homes around the world. Many people drive Japanese cars or motorcycles.

History

You are here!

Kyoto is an ancient city full of amazing temples and other old buildings. After breakfast you set off to explore the city center. You find a tourist brochure that contains a short guide to Japanese history.

Nijo Castle was built in 1603 by a famous shogun named Tokugawa Ieyasu.

The Shogun

The shogun was the head of whichever happened to be the most powerful family in Japan. From the 1190s to the 1860s they ruled in the emperor's name. For the last 200 years of shogun rule, they stopped all contact between Japan and the rest of the world because they feared trade with other countries might lead to an invasion by a foreign power. This left Japan totally cut off from the rest of the world.

Birth of Japan

Japan has been a single country for about 1,600 years. The first Japanese emperor united the country around 400 C.E. An emperor named Kammu founded the city of Kyoto in 794 C.E. Kammu ordered that the city should be laid out in a regular grid pattern. This makes it easy to find your way around.

WORD BANK   samurai Japanese warrior of medieval times

Emperors and warlords

Kyoto was Japan's capital for more than 1,000 years, until the 1860s, when Tokyo became the capital. Nijo Castle is one of the city's most beautiful buildings. This palace did not belong to the emperor but to great warlords called **shoguns**. They were more powerful than the emperor.

Samurai Warriors

Shoguns and other powerful warlords kept armies of warriors called **samurai** to fight with rival families. These soldiers developed a strict code of honor. A samurai would commit suicide, called seppuku, rather than surrender in battle. He would stab himself in the stomach, then a servant would chop off his head.

Survival Tip:
Kyoto has more than 2,000 shrines and temples. Don't even think about trying to visit them all— you'll never have time!

In the 1890s samurai warriors wore thick armor and carried long swords.

---

shogun Japanese military leader. Shoguns ruled Japan for more than 650 years.

Modern Japan

Like most Japanese cities, Kyoto contains a mixture of ancient and modern buildings. The sight of high-rise buildings in Kyoto makes you look at the brochure to find out more about what made Japan the nation it is today.

Japan's Emperors

Japanese people used to believe that their emperors were living gods. Following defeat in World War II, the emperor declared he was not a god. Today's emperor is still head of state, but this is a **ceremonial role**, like the British queen.

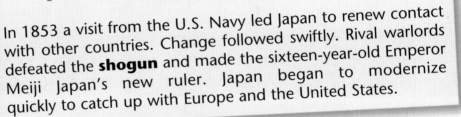

Japan Modernizes

In 1853 a visit from the U.S. Navy led Japan to renew contact with other countries. Change followed swiftly. Rival warlords defeated the **shogun** and made the sixteen-year-old Emperor Meiji Japan's new ruler. Japan began to modernize quickly to catch up with Europe and the United States.

► This old illustration shows the arrival of the U.S. Navy at the harbor at Yedo in 1853.

WORD BANK   ceremonial role duty of a ruler to represent the nation at ceremonies
empire group of countries controlled by one ruler

Recent Years

Around 1900 Japanese leaders began to build an **empire**. They took over land on the Asian mainland, winning wars against China and Russia. In 1941 Japan entered the World War II by launching a surprise attack on the U.S. Navy at Pearl Harbor in Hawaii. In 1945 the United States forced Japan to surrender by dropping huge atomic bombs on the cities of Hiroshima and Nagasaki. After World War II Japan lay in ruins, but it recovered incredibly quickly to become a top industrial nation in just twenty years.

Kamikaze Pilots

During World War II, Japanese **kamikaze** pilots carried out suicide attacks against the U.S. Navy. The pilots flew their planes, often packed with explosives, directly into U.S. ships. A total of 34 ships were sunk by these attacks.

◀ The USS *Bunker Hill* was badly damaged when it was hit by a kamikaze bomb on June 21, 1945.

kamikaze some Japanese pilots in World War II who used their airplanes as bombs to attack enemies

From Kyoto you take the cable car up to nearby Mount Hiei. The view from the top is fantastic with Kyoto surrounded on three sides by mountains. You talk to other onlookers to find out what the rest of Japan is like.

Japan's terrain

Japan is a long, slim country, stretching about 1,500 miles (2,500 kilometers) from north to south. The slender shape of the islands means that you are never far from the sea. Most of inland Japan is mountainous. Lower slopes are covered with forests, and mountain peaks are topped with snow. Towns, factories, and farms are on the narrow **plains** that edge the coasts.

Marathon Monks

The summit of Mount Hiei is covered with temples. The monks here are famous for their harsh discipline. One group, named the "marathon monk," run a 19 mile (30 kilometer) marathon every day for 1,000 days. During the toughest period of 100 days they run 53 miles (85 kilometers) per day! The run is meant to bring the monks closer to nature and their inner thoughts and feelings.

► Cable cars transport people up into the mountains of Honshu.

Quick Facts

Longest river: *the Shinano, 228 miles (367 kilometers) long*
Biggest lake: *Lake Biwa (northeast of Kyoto), covering 259 square miles (672 square kilometers)*
Largest flat area: *the Kanto Plain in eastern Honshu, site of Tokyo, Yokohama, and many other towns*

WORD BANK   plain flat area, sometimes near the coast

Volcanoes and earthquakes

The Japanese are used to volcanoes and earthquakes. The Japanese islands lie along the borders of sections of Earth's crust, called **tectonic plates**. Where these plates meet, they rub against each other, which means that earthquakes and volcanoes are common.

Japan has more than 60 active volcanoes that erupt red-hot lava and clouds of ash from time to time. Earthquakes happen often. Most are so slight they go almost unnoticed, but major earthquakes cause huge destruction.

N
W — E
S

0   300 km

0   200 miles

KEY

☐ Highest peaks
☐ Mid peaks
☐ Lowlands

Deadly Earthquakes

Japan's worst earthquake disaster was the Great Kanto Earthquake of 1923, near Tokyo. It killed more than 100,000 people. In 1995 another major quake rocked the city of Kobe in southwest Honshu. It killed more than 6,300 people and destroyed or badly damaged half a million homes.

Crushed cars are pulled from under a collapsed highway by a giant crane after the earthquake in 1995 in Kobe.
▼

tectonic plate one of the huge slabs of rock that make up Earth's outer layer, which is called the crust

Cherry Blossom Time

The Japanese like to celebrate the changing seasons. Early spring is *hanami* season when people celebrate the blossoming of the cherry trees. Families and friends take time off to picnic under the fruit trees.

Climate

You have been lucky enough to arrive in Japan in spring, when days are mild and sunny. At the top of Mount Hiei you were glad to have your jacket, but things get much warmer as you drop back down to the city again. Do you have the right clothes for visiting the rest of the country?

Because Japan stretches so far north and south, different parts of the country have very different **climates**. In the far north, Hokkaido's weather is icy cold with long, snowy winters and short, cool summers. Central Japan has an average climate, with warm summers and cool winters. Conditions are much hotter in the far south.

People picnic under the pale blossoms during *hanami*, Japan's blossom-viewing festival in spring.

climate regular pattern of weather in an area

Changing seasons

Located in the northern **hemisphere**, Japan's seasons fall at similar times to seasons in the United States and Europe. Clear, sunny weather in early spring is followed by a rainy season lasting up to two months. Summers are hot and sticky. Typhoons (hurricanes) may strike in fall, followed by a spell of mild, clear weather before winter sets in.

Winds called monsoons blow across Japan in opposite directions at different seasons. In summer they blow from the Pacific Ocean, bringing rain to southern and central areas. In winter they blow from mainland Asia, bringing rain and snow to the north and west.

Typhoons

Tropical storms called typhoons (hurricanes) strike Japan between July and November. These huge, spinning storms begin out in the Pacific Ocean, and then sweep inland bringing winds of more than 124 miles per hour (200 kilometers per hour). Torrential rains flatten crops and cause rivers to flood.

It never gets icy cold on Okinawa, an island in the Ryukyu chain.

hemisphere one half of the Earth, which is divided by the equator, an imaginary line around Earth's middle

Food & Culture

Food & Culture

After your trip up Mount Hiei, you're really hungry! You sample the delights of Japanese cooking at a restaurant that is crowded with locals. Japanese people often entertain their guests by eating out rather than cooking at home.

Rice with everything

Rice is the most important food in Japan, eaten at most meals. In fact, the Japanese word for breakfast means "morning rice." Lunch is "noon rice," and supper means — you guessed it—"evening rice." Fish is a common food, as you might expect with so many miles of coast. Sashimi are thin strips of raw fish served with soy sauce and Japanese horseradish.

The Three Os

Eating out in Japan, you're sure to meet the three Os. *Oshibori* are small, damp cloths to wipe your hands and face. *O-hashi* are chopsticks, used instead of knives and forks. At the end of the meal, you will be served *o-cha*—refreshing green tea.

> These men slurp noodles (*soba*), made from buckwheat flour, in a Tokyo noodle bar.

WORD BANK   sushi popular Japanese dish made of flavored patties of rice served with raw fish or vegetables

Slurping noodles

Noodles served in a hot broth make a filling meal. Table manners and politeness are very important in Japan. However, loud slurping sounds are OK when you are eating noodles! Finish off your meal by drinking the broth straight from the bowl.

Seaweed and soybeans are used in many recipes. In the past Japanese people ate little or no meat or dairy products, which made for a low-fat diet. Now these foods are eaten more, as the diet becomes more like the diet in Europe or the United States.

A typical selection of sushi includes raw fish, seaweed, and vegetables.

Types of Restaurants

Many Japanese restaurants serve only one type of food:

Sushi-ya: **Sushi** bars serve patties of vinegar rice topped with raw or cooked fish, vegetables, or seaweed

Soba-ya: Noodle shops serve noodles in a steaming soup, with a meat, fish, egg, or vegetable garnish.

Gift Ideas

Traditional arts and crafts in Japan that make great gifts include:

- *Daruma* dolls: papier-mâché statues, thought to bring good luck
- *Netsuke*: carved toggles, traditionally made of ivory
- Lacquerware: bowls and boxes painted with tree sap that hardens to give a glossy sheen

A traditional lacquerware bowl.

Out and about

The next day you are up early, finding out what is on offer in Japanese cities such as Kyoto. The family you are staying with makes some suggestions about good places to see.

Your first stop is breakfast at one of the fashionable coffee shops now found in city centers in Japan. Visitors sip strong coffee while jazz, rock, or classical music plays. You opt for a traditional breakfast of boiled rice, dried fish, seaweed, soybean soup, and pickles. Afterward you could hit the shops in Kyoto's main shopping district, Gion, in search of souvenirs.

Fancy Packaging

Gift wrapping is an art form in Japan. Any gift you buy will be beautifully wrapped. If you are lucky enough to receive a gift, unwrap it carefully!

WORD BANK Kabuki lively form of drama using song and dance, dating from the 1600s

High drama

How do the Japanese enjoy themselves out and about in the city? Some visit a *pachinko* (pinball) parlor, while others take in a **Kabuki** play. Kabuki is a traditional form of theater—a mix of opera, dance, and music rolled into one. Onlookers throw themselves into the action, cheering heroes and booing villains.

Kabuki is said to have been invented by a beautiful priestess who was also a great dancer. She abandoned the religious life to run away with a **samurai**. Today, however, women are not allowed to perform in kabuki. Men act all of the women's roles.

Pinball Wizards

Pachinko, a form of pinball, is a popular pastime. Bright, noisy *pachinko* parlors are found in every city, and more than half of all Japanese people play regularly. The game is said to have been invented by a Korean factory worker who wanted to find a use for spare ball bearings.

◄ Two Kabuki actors perform a Kabuki play. The plays are about passion, jealousy, and revenge—just like soap operas on television!

pachinko game of pinball played in parlors or arcades in Japan

Shinto Shrines

The entrances to Shinto shrines are marked by a gateway called a *torii*. Visitors **purify** themselves by rinsing their mouth and hands with water. Then they clap three times to attract the gods' attention. They offer a small gift of fruit or money and may pray for health or good luck.

This is a *torii* entrance to a Shinto shrine.

Religion and festivals

You pay a visit to one of Kyoto's most beautiful temples, Kinkakuji. A friendly fellow-visitor tells you about beliefs and festivals in Japan.

Shinto, "the way of the gods," is Japan's oldest religion. People believe that gods called *kami* live in natural places such as rivers, lakes, and mountains. There are millions of these **sacred** spots all over Japan.

Buddhism is another ancient religion that reached Japan about 1,500 years ago. Most Japanese people practice both religions, holding funerals in Buddhist temples and getting married in Shinto shrines.

There are festivals every month of the year in Japan. On Children's Day, also called Boys' Day (May 5) children fly kites in the shape of carp fish. These fish represent strength and determination. On Girls' Day (March 3) girls dress their favorite dolls in miniature silk **kimonos**.

Religious Beliefs

90 percent of Japanese people practice Shinto, while 75 percent are also Buddhists. About 1 percent are Christian, while 9 percent follow other faiths.

WORD BANK Buddhism religion founded in India by a leader known as the Buddha. Buddhism later spread to many parts of Asia.

Kimonos

Kimonos are robes tied at the waist with a sash. Nowadays, few people wear kimonos every day, but both women and men wear them for festivals and special occasions. Made of fine silk, they may be decorated with embroidery.

The Kinkakuji, or Temple of the Golden Pavilion, is one of Kyoto's most beautiful temples. Built by a **shogun** in the 14th century, it is covered with a thin layer of gold leaf.

sacred holy
torii wooden gateway that marks the entrance to a Shinto shrine

Everyday Life

Team Spirit

Team spirit is vital in Japanese companies. A strict **hierarchy** runs from the top bosses down to the junior workers. Everyone wears the same uniform, however, and eats together in the same cafeteria.

In the family you're staying with, you notice that the father always gets home from work late. You ask if this is normal. Apparently, many Japanese people work long hours over six days a week, and only take one or two weeks' holiday a year.

A job for life?

Traditionally, a Japanese worker would stay with the first company he or she started working for until retirement age. Now, however, people are changing jobs more often.

Factory workers stretch and exercise together before starting work in the morning.

▶

WORD BANK   hierarchy way of organizing people or things by grading them by rank

The working day

During the first week in a new job, employees learn company customs, including bowing. People bow to greet their fellow workers, to show thanks, or to say sorry. The deeper the bow, the more respect you show!

Loyalty and politeness are very important in Japanese companies. The day begins with workers bowing to one another. Everyone also does exercises and sings the company song before settling down to work.

After Work

After a long day at the office, Japanese workers often spend the evening together. They may visit an *izakaya*—a cross between a restaurant and a bar. They may go to a bar for a **karaoke** evening to sing along to recorded music. Karaoke was invented in Japan but is now popular in many other countries, too.

This woman performs on stage in a karaoke club in Tokyo.

karaoke form of entertainment, involving singing to prerecorded music

School days

The family you're staying with has two school-age children. They always seem to be doing homework! You ask them about school in Japan.

Schooling begins early for Japanese children. Many begin school at the age of three! Everyone between the ages of six and fifteen goes to school. Ninety percent of children then study at senior high school. One in three go on to college after that.

> These are *Kanji* characters for the words "autumn star."

> These Japanese schoolgirls are studying English.

Japanese writing

Japanese children have to learn four writing systems. *Kanji*, the main script, has thousands of characters. These are little symbols for making up different words. *Hiragana* shows grammar. *Katakana* is used to write foreign words, while *Romanji* uses a Roman alphabet to write Japanese.

WORD BANK   martial art ancient form of self-defense

Working hard

The school day lasts from 8:30 A.M. to 4:30 P.M., Monday to Friday. Students are expected to keep their classroom neat. At the beginning and end of every term, everyone helps give the school a thorough cleaning!

After school, pupils do one to two hours of homework. There are also exams about six times a year! Many students go to private schools called *juku* for extra lessons before exams. No wonder that preparing for exams can be stressful!

▲
Children practice the traditional martial art of judo.

Playing Hard

Sports, art, crafts, and music are all part of the school curriculum. As well as swimming, athletics, baseball, and volleyball, sports such as soccer and rugby are popular. Most children learn one form of **martial art**, such as karate, judo, or **kendo** (fencing), at school.

Sumo Wrestling

Sumo is an ancient sport, dating back at least 1,500 years. Each *rikishi* (wrestler) tries to force his opponent out of the ring, or make him touch the ground with any part of the body except the feet. Sumo wrestlers eat a special diet to put on weight. The average *rikishi* weighs more than 330 pounds (150 kilograms)!

Time off and sports

What do Japanese people do after working hard at work, school, or college? You ask your host family about sports and leisure in Japan.

Playing and watching sports are both popular. **Sumo** wrestling and baseball are national sports. Soccer fever swept Japan in the 1990s. The Japanese also love to play golf. **Martial arts** such as karate, judo, aikido, and **kendo** (fencing) were invented in Japan.

A sumo wrestler uses the *mawashi*, the thick belt worn around the waist, to grasp an opponent during a match.

WORD BANK   bonsai   art of growing miniature trees, a traditional pastime in Japan

Leisure and hobbies

People also enjoy reading books, newspapers, and comics. More comics are sold in Japan than in any other country!

Japanese people are enthusiastic gardeners. Even in crowded cities, people tend a small yard or window box. **Bonsai,** or miniature trees, can be grown indoors. Many children like *purikura* (print club) machines. These machines take photos of children and their friends in fun poses. The photos are then made into tiny stickers that end up everywhere!

Baseball

Yakyu (baseball) reached Japan from the United States in the late 1800s. Teams from the two major leagues, the Central and Pacific Leagues, battle it out in summer. The field is smaller than in the United States and does not have a standard size. The rules are a little different, too.

Bonsai trees grow less than 3 feet (1 meter) tall. The tiny branches are carefully pruned and wired to make a beautiful shape.

sumo form of wrestling traditional in Japan

Travel & Cities

Speeding Bullets

Japan's "bullet trains," or *shinkansen*, were developed in the 1960s. These trains race at 170 miles (275 kilometers) per hour between cities. The Kyoto to Tokyo line extends from Kyushu in the south to northern Honshu. You get a great view of Mount Fuji as you speed past!

After a few days in Kyoto, you are eager to see more of the country. You ask at the tourist office about the best way to travel. Japan has one of the fastest, most reliable transportation networks in the world.

Air travel

Japan has more than 170 airports, including some that are international. Some of the most modern, such as Osaka, are built on artificial islands in the sea, because there is so little flat land in Japan. Jumbo jets are used for flights around Japan because so many people travel by air.

Some bullet trains have two decks. Seats on the more expensive top deck even have their own television!

WORD BANK   *shinkansen* Japan's high-speed trains, also called "bullet trains"

Road and rail

Japan's road network is modern, with most roads going around the coast. Some roads go through tunnels under the mountains. Motorists drive on the left-hand side of the road. Buses connect the major cities, while taxis are used inside towns.

Four different types of trains run on Japan's rail network. The faster they go, the more you pay! Maglev, short for magnetic levitation, is a new development. These are trains that have no wheels. Instead, magnets on the train and track push away from each other, which makes the train float above the rail.

Record-Breakers

Since the 1980s, some ultra-long bridges and tunnels have been built to carry cars or trains between Japan's four main islands. The world's longest single-span road bridge, Akashi Kaikyo Bridge, links Honshu island to Shikoku island. The Seikan Tunnel between Honshu and Hokkaido island is the world's longest rail tunnel. It is almost 34 miles (54 kilometers) long.

The Akashi Kaikyo Bridge spans a huge 6,529 feet (1,990 meters).

29

You are here!

Tokyo: Japan's capital

The bullet train pulls into Tokyo Station. You have arrived in Japan's capital, one of the world's largest cities! It is home to a quarter of Japan's population.

Eastern capital

Located on the densely populated Kanto Plain, Tokyo's name means "eastern capital." This was the home of the **shoguns** that ruled Japan for hundreds of years. Most of Tokyo's architecture is modern, with **futuristic** buildings such as the Stark Building. Most old buildings have either been destroyed by fire, the Great Kanto Earthquake in 1923, or by bombing during World War II.

Tsukiji Fish Market

Tokyo's fish market is said to be the world's busiest and most exciting. The tuna auction is in full swing by 5:30 A.M., so you've got to get up early! Stalls also sell crabs, shrimps, and other shellfish. Nearby **sushi** bars serve the freshest sushi in Japan.

▶ Ginza is Tokyo's main shopping district. Shoppers in search of a bargain jostle **commuters** during rush hours.

Sightseeing in Tokyo

Many of Tokyo's top sights lie just a short distance from the station. The grounds of the Imperial Palace hold the Science Museum and the National Museum of Modern Art. A short way to the north you will find Ueno Park, a large park with a zoo and boating lake as well as more museums.

Outside the city center, most streets do not have names, so it's hard for taxi drivers to find their way around! But you can call for advice using one of the bright yellow tourist phones if you get lost.

"Rooms" in a capsule hotel are very cosy! They measure just 6 feet long by 3 feet wide by 3 feet tall (2 meters by 1 meter by 1 meter).

Capsule Hotels

Space is so cramped in downtown Tokyo that some hotels have rooms no larger than big lockers! These hotels are called "capsule hotels." There's space just for a bed, television screen, radio, and one guest!

Fact File: Tokyo

Population (in 2000): 12,064,000 people
Area: 844 square miles (2,187 square kilometers)
Founded: During the 1400s, when it was known as Edo. It has been Japan's capital since 1868.

Island Shrine

The island shrine of Miyajima lies in the bay at Hiroshima. The whole island is a **sacred** site and deer roam free here. The island's curving gateway, or *torii,* is one of the best-known sights in Japan.

Japan's cities

Tokyo is just one of Japan's many great cities. You ask at the tourist office about other cities worth a visit.

Sapporo, on the island of Hokkaido, is a great place for skiing. Nara is an ancient city, similar to Kyoto, with hundreds of temples. Yokohoma on the Kanto **Plain** is Japan's biggest port, while Nagoya and Kobe are busy industrial centers.

Some tourists visit Hiroshima in western Honshu. The city was destroyed when the United States dropped an atomic bomb on it in 1945 at the end of World War II. There are several monuments to the war. The Peace Park has a flame that will only be put out when all nuclear weapons have been destroyed.

The famous "floating gateway" of Miyajima stands in the bay.

Fact Box
Japan's largest cities in order of population size are: Tokyo, Yokohama, Osaka, Nagoya, Sapporo, Kyoto, Kobe, and Fukuoka.

Old and new in Osaka

You decide to head for Osaka in southern Honshu. It is Japan's third-largest city and home to the country's famous puppet theater, called *bunraku*. There is also a beautiful castle that dates from the 16th century. Nearby, Panasonic Square attracts young people, with the latest computer games on display. You try out a virtual reality game and then tour the city's waterways by boat.

You are here!

TOKYO

Osaka

N
W — E
S

0   300 km

0   200 miles

Puppet Theater

Bunraku, or puppet theater, dates back over 400 years. The puppets act out new plays or traditional stories. The puppeteers are not hidden but work the puppets so skillfully that you hardly notice them. The *bunraku* puppets are about half life-size. They are very realistic. Their eyes can be made to move, their eyebrows rise in surprise, their mouths open and shut, and their hands and arms can move gracefully.

Like many Japanese cities, Osaka is a mixture of the ancient and the modern. Gleaming skyscrapers dwarf the old castle.

Cramming on the Trains

Trains and subways in Japanese cities are packed with **commuters** during rush hours. Special officials, called *oshiya* (pushers), are employed to cram as many people as possible on to every train!

Urban life

In Osaka you opt to stay in another *minshuku* (family-run guest house). It's the best way to get a taste of real city life!

Crowded centers

More than three-quarters of Japan's population live in towns on the coastal **plains**, such as Osaka. As in Tokyo, Osaka's streets are very crowded during rush hour. Highways that pass over other highways help prevent traffic jams in city centers. However, parking and pollution are still a problem. The best way to get to work is to walk or bike to the nearest station and take the train or subway.

City homes

Homes in city centers are small, and there are just four rooms being usual for a family with two children. The kitchen and dining room are often combined, with two bedrooms plus a main living space.

No one wears shoes indoors. Outdoor shoes are always left in the *genkan*, a hallway, which is often on a lower level. People wear slippers in the house except in rooms with *tatami* matting. Here people just wear socks. Special slippers are provided for the bathroom.

Bath Time

Bath time in Japan involves a relaxing soak in a bathtub filled with piping-hot water. You soap yourself down or shower first to get clean before jumping into the tub, which the whole family takes turn using.

This is a traditional Japanese bedroom.

Subway Systems

Tokyo, Yokohama, Osaka, Kyoto, Nagoya, Sapporo, Kobe, and Fukuoka all have subway systems.

Rural Life

Family Sizes

Until about 50 years ago, Japanese families were a lot larger. Parents, children, and grandparents all lived under one roof. Grandparents took care of young children while parents worked. This is still common in the countryside, but it is rare in cities today.

This large family lives together in rural Japan.

N
W E
S

0   300 km

0   200 miles

Ogimachi

TOKYO

You are here!

As a break from city life, you decide to relax for a few days in the country. You head for the village of Ogimachi in the Japan Alps in northern Honshu, where the pace of life is slower.

WORD BANK   thatched describes a roof made of dry straw or reeds

A mountain village

Ogimachi is a traditional farming village with tall, **thatched** houses. The roofs are steep so that the snow can slide off them. Snow still lingers on the surrounding mountains, and the air is clear and cold.

Villages such as Ogimachi are quiet by day. Most adults travel to nearby towns to work, though some people work in the fields or at local crafts. Older children also go to school in nearby towns.

Plans for the future

You rent a bicycle to explore the countryside. At a local temple you meet a group of teenagers on a school trip who are eager to practice their English. You ask about their plans when they leave school. Some cannot wait to escape to a big city. Others want to stay in the country. Today, new technology such as the Internet is making it easier for people to work at home, wherever they live.

People live on the first floor of tall village houses. The top floor is traditionally used for storage and craftwork.

Keeping Warm

The climate in the mountains is colder than in the lowlands. Country homes are usually heated with oil stoves or electric heaters. In winter, people sit around the *kotatsu*—a low table with a heater underneath. They warm their legs under the quilt that covers the table.

Silk Farming

People raise silkworms in mulberry orchards in central Honshu. The silkworms spin silken cocoons just before they pupate (change from a caterpillar to an adult moth).The threads are harvested and woven to make silk.

Farming and fishing

Ogimachi sits in a narrow valley, which you explore by bicycle. Vegetable gardens, rice fields, and small flower plots fill the valley bottom.

Agriculture

Most fields in Japan are small, like those around Ogimachi. Some farmers use high-tech machinery, others use simple tools. Most farming is now done on weekends, with people doing office or factory work during the week. Rice is the main crop. It is grown in **paddy fields**, which are kept flooded with water. Farmers also grow wheat, barley, tobacco, vegetables, tea, and fruits such as oranges, apples, and pears.

On hillsides, like this one in Wakayama, the land is stepped to make flat terraces to grow rice.

paddy field field used to grow rice that can be flooded at certain times of the year

Fishing industry

You catch a bus to the nearby coast where fishing boats bob in the harbor. Fish, shellfish, and seaweed are all a big part of the Japanese diet.

Japan's fishing boats search local waters and also the world's oceans for tuna, salmon, cod, sardines, and shellfish. The country nets one-eighth of the world's total fish catch. Carp and trout are raised in tanks, while bream and tuna are farmed on coasts.

Cooking with Tofu

Tofu is a nutritious, fat-free food. Tofu is made by soaking and grinding soybeans and then removing the liquid from the milky mixture so it sets. Slabs of tofu may be boiled, grilled, or fried. Recipes include delicious *yu-dofu*. Heat the tofu in water flavored with seaweed, then serve it with grated ginger, chopped spring onions, soy sauce, and flakes of dried fish.

These are Japanese fishing boats moored in a harbor in Kyushu.

Tourism & Travel

Top Attractions of Japan's National Parks

- Daisetsuzan, Hokkaido: Japan's largest national park, great hiking country
- Fuji-Hakone-Izu, Honshu: lakes, unspoiled beaches, volcanoes including Mount Fuji
- Aso-Kuji, Kyushu: smoking volcanoes, bubbling pools
- Inland sea between Honshu and Shikoku: rugged coastline, pine-covered islands

In Ogimachi you are staying in a *ryokan*—a traditional inn where both Japanese and western tourists stay. You ask the other guests for tips on good places to visit in Japan.

Island attractions

So far, you've seen only parts of mainland Honshu, but there's plenty to see on the other main islands. Each has its own character and attractions. Hokkaido in the north has the largest wilderness areas. Shikoku in the south is famous for its temples, while Kyushu has active volcanoes and hot springs.

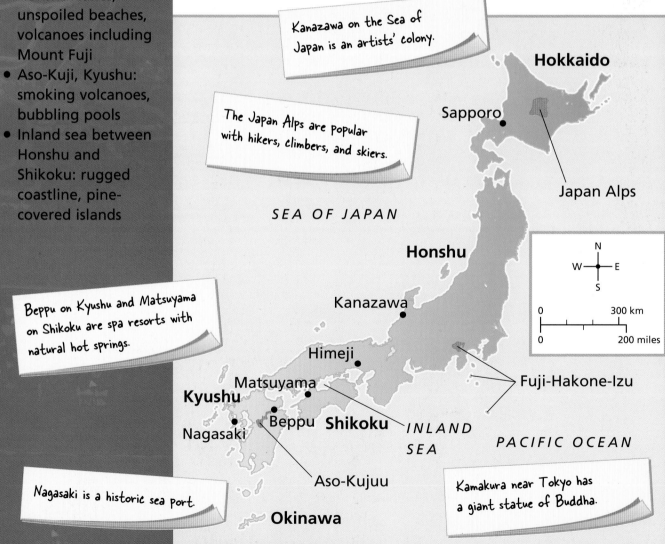

Kanazawa on the Sea of Japan is an artists' colony.

The Japan Alps are popular with hikers, climbers, and skiers.

Beppu on Kyushu and Matsuyama on Shikoku are spa resorts with natural hot springs.

Nagasaki is a historic sea port.

Kamakura near Tokyo has a giant statue of Buddha.

Hokkaido

Sapporo

Japan Alps

SEA OF JAPAN

Honshu

Kanazawa

Fuji-Hakone-Izu

Himeji

Matsuyama

Kyushu

Beppu   **Shikoku**

Nagasaki

INLAND SEA

PACIFIC OCEAN

Aso-Kujuu

Okinawa

N W E S

0   300 km

0   200 miles

Natural wonders

Japan's national parks protect areas of natural beauty, including volcanoes, hot springs, crater lakes, wetlands, rugged coastlines, and remote islands.

In the far south, the Ryukyu and Bonin island chains have a warm and wet **climate**. There are sandy beaches and excellent snorkeling in the clear blue waters off the coral reefs.

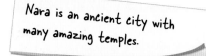

Nara is an ancient city with many amazing temples.

The Castle of the White Crane at Himeji, western Honshu, is one of Japan's most beautiful castles.

Sapporo, Hokkaido, is a winter sports center. In February, the Snow Festival here has amazing ice and snow sculptures.

41

Stay or Go Home?

Hot Springs

Take a dip in one of Japan's famous *onsen* (hot springs), where the water is heated by underground volcanic activity. The warm, bubbling waters relieve aches and pains. As in an indoor bath, you must soap and rinse first before hopping in.

You have seen a bit of Japan now: the sights of Kyoto, Tokyo, and Osaka and the countryside around Ogimachi. However, there is lots more to see and do! It's decision time. Do you hop on a plane and head for home or stay and sample more of Japan?

Skiing or paddling?

Your friends at the inn at Ogimachi put together a list of must-do activities. One of the top priorities is to go snowboarding or skiing in the Japan Alps or on Hokkaido before all the snow melts! At Ogi on Sado Island in northern Honshu, local women paddle washtub boats around the bay to collect shellfish. You can rent a washtub, too, but steering is tricky!

►

Snowboarding in Hokkaido is becoming a very popular pastime.

crane type of long-legged water bird

Wildlife and hiking

You have seen a little of Japan's wildlife, which includes graceful **cranes** that attract their mates by dancing. You make a note to visit the island of Shodo-shima in the Inland Sea, to see the wild macaques, or snow monkeys, showing off. Snow monkeys are now an endangered species, although special wildlife parks have been set up around Japan to keep them from going extinct.

For the Japanese, climbing **sacred** Mount Fuji is a once-in-a-lifetime experience. The climbing season is July and August. You can hike all the way from the bottom or cheat by taking the bus halfway up!

In some parts of Japan, macaques keep warm in freezing cold weather by bathing in hot springs.

A hostess prepares tea during a tea ceremony.

The Tea Ceremony

The best way to relax in Japan is to go to a tea ceremony. This ritual takes place in a tea pavilion in a beautiful garden. The guests chat while the hostess prepares special green tea. The ceremony can take up to four hours!

Find Out More

World Wide Web

If you want to find out more about Japan, you can search the Internet using keywords such as these:

• Japan
• Shinano River
• Tokyo

You can also find your own keywords by using headings or words from this book. Try using a search directory such as yahooligans.com.

Are there ways for an eager Destination Detective to find out more about Japan? Yes! Check out the books and Internet search tips listed below:

Further Reading

Dean, Arlan. *Samurai: Warlords of Japan*. Danbury, Conn.: Children's Press, 2005.

Green, Jen. *Nations of the World: Japan*. Chicago: Raintree, 2001.

Haslam, Andrew. *Make It Work: Japan*. Minnetonka, Minn.: Two-Can Publishing, 2000.

Kalman, Bobbie. *Japan: The People*. New York: Crabtree Publishing, 2000.

Richardson, Hazel. *Life in Ancient Japan*. New York: Crabtree Publishing, 2005.

Movies

Spirited Away (2001)
This animated film is directed by Hayao Miyazaki. A miserable ten-year-old girl who is moving house with her parents stumbles into the mysterious world of the Japanese gods.

The Seven Samurai (1953)
Directed by Akira Kurosawa, this is a classic film about Japan's medieval warriors.

Time Line

about 400 C.E.
A powerful family called the Yamoto unite Japan to become the emperors.

400s
Chinese ideas and systems of writing influence Japan's culture.

552
The Buddhist religion reaches Japan from China and Korea.

646
The emperor's power is strengthened by a set of laws called the Taika Reform.

710
Japan's capital is built at Nara.

794
Kyoto becomes the capital of Japan.

1192
Yoritomo, head of the Minamoto clan, becomes the first **shogun.**

1270s–1280s
Mongol forces invading Japan are driven back by a typhoon, which the Japanese call a **kamikaze** (divine wind).

1543
Portuguese sailors are the first Europeans to visit Japan.

1603
Tokugawa Ieyasu becomes shogun. The Tokugawa clan remains in power for the next 264 years, ruling Japan from Edo (now Tokyo).

1630s
Japan cuts off all contact with the outside world.

1853–1854
Commodore Matthew Perry of the United States persuades Japan to renew contact with the outside world.

1868
The rule of the shoguns is overthrown. The traditional power of Japan's emperors is restored under Emperor Meiji. Tokyo becomes capital of Japan.

1894–1895
Japan wins a war against China over Korea.

1905
Japan wins a war against Russia.

1923
The Great Kanto Earthquake devastates Tokyo, Yokohama, and other cities on the Kanto Plain.

1937
Japan invades China.

1941
Japan bombs U.S. ships at Pearl Harbor in Hawaii and enters World War II on the side of Germany. The United States enters the war on the opposite side, called the Allies.

1945
Japan surrenders after U.S. aircraft drop atomic bombs on the cities of Hiroshima and Nagasaki. U.S. and Allied forces take over Japan.

1952
U.S. and Allied forces withdraw from Japan.

1956
Japan joins the United Nations.

1960s
Japan's economy booms.

1989
Emperor Hirohito dies and is succeeded by his son Akihito.

1992
Recession (economic slowdown) affects Japan's economy.

1995
The Kobe earthquake kills more than 6,300 people.

2001
Unichiro Koizumi becomes prime minister of Japan.

Japan: Facts & Figures

The Japanese flag has a white background with a red circle in the center. The white represents honesty and purity, and the red disc is a sun symbol meaning brightness, sincerity, and warmth. The Japanese flag first became the country's national flag in 1868.

People and Places

- Population: 127.4 million.
- Mount Aso National Park on the small island of Jumamoto is one of the world's largest areas of volcanic activity.
- Average life expectancy: 81.5 years

What's in a Name?

- Japan's official name is Nippon, or Nihon, meaning "Source of the Sun."
- The national flag of Japan is known as the Nisshohki or Hinomaru, which means "sun disc" in Japanese.

Food Facts

- The average Japanese person eats more than 154 pounds (69 kilograms) of fish per year—almost half a pound (227 grams) per day!
- Never stick chopsticks upright into your bowl of rice, or other food, as this is an old Japanese custom for offering food, especially rice, to the dead.

Money Matters

- Japan's economic output is huge, second only to the United States.
- Average earnings:
Men: US$37,345 (£21,291)
Women: US$16,601 (£9,465)

Glossary

bonsai art of growing miniature trees, a traditional pastime in Japan

Buddhism religion founded in India by a leader known as the Buddha. Buddhism later spread to many parts of Asia.

ceremonial role duty of a ruler to represent the nation at ceremonies

climate regular pattern of weather in an area

commuter worker who travels to his or her job, often in a city

crane type of long-legged water bird

empire group of countries controlled by one country

futon mattress that can be rolled up when not in use

futuristic modern-looking

hemisphere one-half of the Earth, which is divided by the equator, an imaginary line around Earth's middle

hierarchy way of organizing people or things by grading them by rank

Kabuki lively form of drama using song and dance, dating from the 1600s

kamikaze some Japanese pilots in World War II who used their airplanes as bombs to attack enemies

karaoke form of entertainment, involving singing to prerecorded music

kendo martial art of fencing, using bamboo swords

kimono robe with wide sleeves, which is the traditional dress of Japanese men and women

martial art ancient form of self-defense

paddy field field used to grow rice, which can be flooded at certain times of the year

pachinko game of pinball played in parlors or arcades in Japan

pagoda tall, tower-like temple with several layers of curving roofs

plain flat area, sometimes near the coast

purify cleanse or make something clean

sacred holy

samurai Japanese warrior of medieval times

shinkansen Japan's high-speed trains, also called "bullet trains"

Shinto ancient Japanese religion, meaning "way of the gods"

shogun Japanese military leader. Shoguns ruled Japan for more than 650 years.

sumo form of wrestling traditional in Japan

sushi popular Japanese dish made of flavored patties of rice served with raw fish or vegetables

thatched describes a roof made of dry straw or reeds

tectonic plate one of the huge slabs of rock that make up Earth's outer layer, which is called the crust

torii wooden gateway that marks the entrance to a Shinto shrine

yen currency of Japan

Index